**A FIDELER/GATEWAY
STORY OF AMERICA BOOK**

STORY OF TRANSPORTATION

Wilma Wilson Cain

Gateway
Press, Inc.

Grand Rapids, Michigan

HISTORICAL ADVISOR

Clifton R. Fox
Department of History
Michigan State University

EDITORIAL AND DESIGN STAFF

Manuscript

Margaret Fisher Hertel

Jerry E. Jennings

Mary Mitus

Marion H. Smith

Art

Lee Brown

Ellen Osborn

Copyright 1988, Gateway Press, Inc.
Grand Rapids, Michigan

LIBRARY OF CONGRESS CATALOG CARD NUMBER: 87-081355
ISBN: 0-934291-24-1

Earlier Edition Copyright, The Fideler Company, 1966

Jun 13, 88
G. PE 1127
f. 9793 - Qop 2

Grateful acknowledgment is made to the following for permission to use the illustrations found in this book:

American Pioneer Trails Association, Inc.: Page 37.

Association of American Railroads: Pages 80 and 82.

Automobile Manufacturers Association: Page 105.

Ballou's Pictorial, March 10, 1855: Page 58.

Baltimore and Ohio Railroad Company: Pages 77, 78, 79, and 81.

Bethlehem Shipbuilding Corporation, Ltd.: Page 63.

Bettmann Archive: Pages 96, 101, and 113.

Bicycle Institute of America: Page 103.

Bostonian Society: Page 111.

Brown Brothers: Pages 54, 65, 66, and 72.

Bureau of Public Roads: Pages 9, 18, 26, 27, 28, 29, 32, 39, 40, and 48.

Carnival Cruise Lines — Photo by Al Wolfe Associates, Inc.: Page 115.

Chicago Historical Society: Page 38.

Chicago Transit Authority: Page 94.

City Art Museum of St. Louis: Page 45.

Culver Service: Pages 69, 87, and 88.

Dallas-Fort Worth International Airport: Page 122.

Devaney: Pages 93 and 116.

The Fideler Company: Pages 10, 11, 12, 14, 15, 22, 42, 43, and 62.

Ford Motor Company: Page 107.

Frederick Way, Jr.: Pages 71 and 73.

Gendreau: Pages 55 and 60.

General Motors Corporation: Pages 106 and 109.

Grand Rapids Area Transit Authority, courtesy of La Bakk Studio, Ltd.: Page 98.

Handy Studios: Page 36.

Knox College: Pages 47 and 74.

Lee Brown: Cover.

Library of Congress: Pages 24, 31, 84, 85, 86, 99, and 102.

Maryland Historical Society: Page 30.

Mattutuck Historical Society: Page 19.

Metropolitan Museum of Art: Page 68.

Michigan Travel Commission: Page 53.

NASA, Johnson Space Center: Page 7.

National Archives: Page 118.

National Life Insurance Company: Pages 13 and 16.

Nebraska Department of Roads: Page 108.

Newberry Library: Page 67.

New York Central System: Page 76.

New York City Transit Authority: Page 97.

New-York Historical Society: Pages 50, 64, 92, and 112.

New York Public Library: Pages 17, 25, 49, and 91.

New York State Department of Commerce Photo: Page 114.

Old Print Shop, Inc.: Pages 20 and 70.

Paramount Pictures Corporation: Page 83.

Peabody Museum of Salem: Pages 21 and 56.

Picturesque America, N.Y. 1872 — Engraving by A.R. Waud: Page 44.

Roberts: Pages 89 and 104.

San Antonio Light — Photo by Byron Samford: Page 110.

Sanborn Studio: Page 41.

Smithsonian Institution: Pages 3, 23, 59, and 100.

Stanford University Press: Page 34.

Stanley M. Arthurs: Page 46.

Texas State Department of Highways and Public Transportation: Page 90.

Trans World Airlines, Inc.: Page 120.

Tulane University: Page 75.

United Airlines Audio Visual Services: Page 123.

United States Department of Transportation, Federal Aviation Administration: Page 121.

United States Forest Service: Page 8.

United States National Museum: Page 117.

Valentine Museum: Page 95.

Wells Fargo Bank: Page 35.

Wide World Photos, Inc.: Page 119.

Wisconsin State Capitol: Page 33.

CONTENTS

Introduction 6

1 Indian Canoes 9

2 Travel in Colonial America 15

3 The Colonists Sail the Sea 20

4 Early Roads in America 25

5 The Stagecoach 31

6 Covered Wagons 36

7 Flatboats on the Rivers.......................... 43

8 Canalboat Days 48

9 Sailing Ships 55

10 Clipper Ships and Schooners 59

11 The First Steamboats 64

12 River Steamers 70

13 The Coming of the Railroad 76

14 Railroads Unite the Nation 83

15 Transportation in the City 91

16 The Bicycle..................................... 99

17 Automobiles 105

18 Ocean Liners and Submarines 111

19 Travel by Air 117

Glossary 124

Index 127

INTRODUCTION

One summer night in 1983, a space shuttle stood ready for lift-off at Kennedy Space Center, in Florida. The giant spacecraft had three main parts. One was a fuel tank five stories high. Attached to the fuel tank were two powerful booster rockets that would lift the shuttle into space. Also attached to the fuel tank was a triangle-shaped spaceplane called an orbiter. Inside the orbiter were five astronauts.

At 2:32 a.m. the space shuttle roared upward. High above the earth's surface, the booster rockets separated from the fuel tank and dropped gently back to earth by parachute. They would be used again to boost another shuttle into space. Then the empty fuel tank separated from the orbiter and dropped in pieces into the ocean.

The orbiter continued on to circle round and round the earth. It contained everything the astronauts needed to stay comfortable on their journey. After almost a week in space, the astronauts prepared to return to earth. Two engines were started on the orbiter to slow it down. It glided swiftly back toward earth like a paper airplane and landed on the long runway of Edwards Air Force Base in California. From there, it was loaded on the back of a huge jet airplane and flown back to Kennedy Space Center where it would be made ready for another flight into space.

This was the eighth time a space shuttle had made a successful flight. For more than thirty years, scientists had been working on ways for people to travel into space and back. The first spacecraft were too expensive and inconvenient to be practical for regular travel. Their rockets could be used only once. When the early spacecraft returned to earth they had to splash down into the ocean.

6

However, the space shuttle's rockets could be used over again. Also, it landed like an ordinary airplane.

Space travel is still expensive and risky. In 1986, a teacher named Christa McAuliffe and six other people were killed in a space shuttle flight. However, someday people may be able to travel into space and back as easily as we travel from one country to another.

A hundred years ago, space travel would have seemed like an impossible dream. Even the idea of traveling in an airplane would have seemed impossible. This book explores the story of transportation in our country. It begins before the time that colonists from Europe came to North America. The people who lived here at that early time were the American Indians. Our story of transportation in America begins with Indian canoes.

A space shuttle is lifted off the earth by giant rockets.

Traveling by canoe was faster and more convenient than journeying through dense forests.

1 Indian Canoes

A birch-bark canoe glides silently down a stream. In the stern kneels an Indian. He guides the canoe along with a single wooden paddle. Suddenly the calm waters of the stream change to rushing rapids. Carefully, the Indian steers his canoe past rocks and whirlpools into the quiet waters beyond. Soon the stream becomes very shallow. The canoe skims easily across water only six inches deep.

* Please see glossary

9

Dense forests made travel difficult for Indians and colonists in Colonial America.

Birch-bark canoes. Indians used bark from birch trees for building strong, lightweight canoes.

A little farther on, a waterfall blocks the Indian's journey. He paddles to the bank and pulls the canoe out of the water. Carrying it over his head, he walks to the calm waters below the falls. There he continues his journey down the stream.

Indians traveled in birch-bark canoes on the lakes and rivers of America long before colonists from Europe came to this country. Travel by water was faster and more convenient than journeying through the forests that covered the land.

Each Indian tribe had its own style of birch-bark canoe. These canoes were of different sizes, varying from ten to sixty feet in length. They were long and narrow with high, pointed ends. Birch-barks were strong and could carry heavy loads. Yet they were also light in weight.

It took great skill to build a birch-bark canoe. The Indians carefully peeled long strips of bark from birch trees. They sewed these strips together with long, threadlike roots. The frame of the canoe was made from strips of wood. (See picture on page 10.) More roots were used to sew the bark to the frame. Finally, hot pitch*

Dugout canoes were made of hollowed logs. These were first burned out and then scraped smooth.

was poured on the seams and cracks to make the canoe watertight.

Indians living in the southeastern part of the country did not use birch-bark canoes, for very few birch trees grew there. Instead, they used dugout canoes. To make one of these, they selected a log that was from fifteen to thirty feet long and about three feet thick. Then they burned out the inside of the log and scraped it smooth with shells and stones. The finished canoe was very heavy. Indians did not try to carry dugouts overland from one stream to another.

Soon after the colonists came to America, they began using canoes for transportation. At first they bought birch-bark canoes from the Indians. However, these lightweight canoes upset very

Dugouts were used by Indians who lived in the Southeast, for very few birch trees grew there.

Many colonists used dugouts because these heavier canoes upset less easily than birchbarks.

easily. The colonists had so much trouble with them that they began to use dugout canoes. They traveled more slowly in dugouts, but there was less chance of turning over.

French explorers and fur traders also traveled in Indian canoes. While English colonists were settling along the Atlantic coast, the French were exploring much of the interior of North America. Many of these explorers traveled into this region in birch-bark canoes. Some of the French were fur traders who lived near the Great Lakes. Each summer the traders loaded their furs in canoes. Then they paddled along the shores of the Great Lakes and down the St. Lawrence River* to the town of Montreal, where they sold the furs.

Today, many people still enjoy canoeing. Some modern canoes look much like those the Indians were using when the colonists first came to America.

Fur traders used birch-bark canoes on the Great Lakes and the St. Lawrence River.*

Sharing a horse. Horses were so scarce in Colonial America that two people often rode together.

2 Travel in Colonial America

The first colonists in America did very little traveling. Huge trees and thick bushes covered the land around their tiny settlements. There were no roads through these dense forests. Also, the colonists had no horses, no carts, and no carriages. When they did

Delivering mail. Postriders on horseback carried mail regularly from colony to colony.

travel, it was usually by water. Some colonists paddled over lakes and rivers in Indian canoes. Many of the families who lived along a river or the ocean owned small, wooden boats.

Horses were brought to the colonies early in the seventeenth century. However, they could not travel along the narrow trails through the forests. Gradually, the trails were widened and people were able to go from one colony to another on horseback. In the latter part of the seventeenth century, travelers were riding horseback between Boston and Philadelphia. Postriders, who carried mail, traveled regularly from colony to colony on horseback.

16

In early colonial times horses were so scarce that two people often rode together on one horse. One person sat on the saddle, and the other rode on a padded cushion behind. On a long journey, four people sometimes shared the same horse. At the start of the trip, two rode off on the horse and the other two began walking. After a few miles, the riders tied the horse beside the road and continued on foot. When the other two persons reached the horse, they rode for a few miles, passing their friends on the way. Then they left the horse beside the road and began walking again. Thus the four took turns riding and walking.

By the end of the seventeenth century, carts, coaches, and carriages were being used by the colonists. Farmers used two-wheeled

An oxcart. Many farmers used two-wheeled carts pulled by oxen to carry their products to market.

oxcarts to carry their farm products to town. These carts were very awkward and heavy. Many of them had solid wooden wheels. In the cities, a few families owned four-wheeled coaches that were drawn by two horses. Some colonists used two-wheeled carriages pulled by one horse. Many of these were open. Others had leather tops. These small carriages were often painted in bright shades of red, yellow, or blue.

The hard-working colonists had little time for pleasure trips in the summer. Winter was the time for riding across the country-side to visit friends and relatives. Horse-drawn sleighs could travel

A one-horse carriage. Some of the colonists traveled in small, two-wheeled carriages.

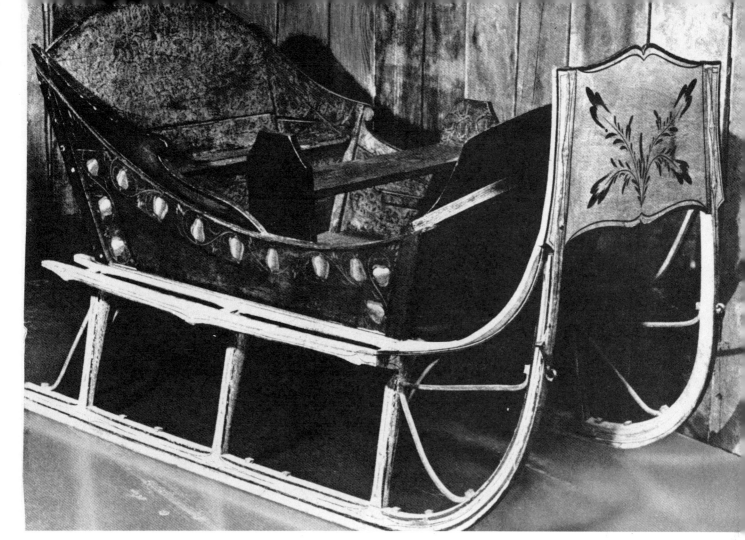

A sleigh. Many colonists made their own sleighs and painted them in bright colors.

swiftly over the snow-covered ground. Frozen streams and rivers made smooth winter highways.

Farm families sometimes traveled to market in large sleighs. In the sleigh, with the mother and children, were piles of cheeses, bunches of dried herbs, and great bundles of vegetables. The father walked alongside in the snow. Colonial families often made their own sleighs and painted them in bright colors.

Harpooning a whale. Many men in the colonies made their living on the sea as whalers.

3 The Colonists Sail the Sea

One breezy day in 1760 a crowd of quiet, anxious-looking people stood on a wharf in the harbor of Nantucket.* They were watching men raise the sails on a tall-masted ship anchored near the dock. Soon the sails billowed out in the wind, and the anchor was lifted. The people on shore began to wave good-by. Men on board the ship moved close to the rail. They were not sure they would ever see their families and friends in Nantucket again.

These sailors were starting on a dangerous search for whales. Their whaling voyage would take them far out on the Atlantic

Ocean. On the deck of their ship was a large boiler. In it they would melt whale blubber* to make oil for lamps and street lights. It might be many months before the ship would return to Nantucket loaded with barrels of whale oil.

Fishermen and traders, as well as whalers, sailed from the ports of Colonial America. Sturdy, wooden ships took the fishermen far out to sea, and brought them safely home again. They carried traders to many distant lands. Most of these strong ships were built by hand in the shipyards located near almost every port in America.

The first shipyard in the American colonies was built in Massachusetts in 1629, only nine years after the founding of Plymouth Colony. By 1700, the colonists had built many shipyards along

The "Iris" was built in a New England shipyard. There were many good shipyards in the colonies.

the coast of New England. Much good lumber for shipbuilding came from the dense forests around the early settlements. Oak, yellow pine, and spruce trees were cut into lumber for hulls and decks. There were many tall, white pine trees from which ship-builders made straight masts for sailing ships. The colonists built ships so well and so inexpensively that their shipyards were known all over the world.

The early colonists built small, one-masted fishing boats. In these boats they sailed hundreds of miles off the New England coast to catch cod,* mackerel,* and other fish. The huge catches of fish which they brought back were cleaned, salted, and spread

Building a ship. Oak, yellow pine, and spruce trees were used to make hulls and decks.

A model of a schooner.* The first ship of this kind was completed in New England in 1713.

in the sun to dry. Large shipments of dried fish were sold to merchants in Europe.

During the eighteenth century, many fishermen began using a new type of ship called the schooner.* The first schooner was built in the small New England village of Gloucester. It was completed in 1713. These first schooners had two masts and two large sails. Fewer men were needed to sail a schooner than were needed on the earlier fishing boats.

The colonists also built ships to carry cargo and passengers along the Atlantic coast and across the ocean. Passengers who traveled on these trading vessels often had a long, slow journey.

23

The ship did not have a planned route. Its captain sailed from port to port, buying cargoes of dried fish, rum, molasses, and other goods. Sometimes he stayed in one port for many days looking for goods to buy. Then he sailed on to other ports to sell his cargo. Often passengers spent weeks at sea waiting for the right winds to blow the ship on its way to a port. They might have to stay on the ship for months before the captain decided to sail to the city they wished to visit.

A fishing schooner. Colonial fishermen sailed for many miles to catch cod* and other fish.

An early road. Many of the first roads in America were made by widening Indian trails.

4 Early Roads in America

Many of the early roads in America began as Indian trails. Indians had made these narrow paths as they walked through the dense forests from one waterway to another. When the first colonists came to America, they traveled on foot over many of these trails. Gradually, they widened them by cutting away the trees and bushes on either side. The wider trails then served as roads.

25

A corduroy* road. Logs were sometimes laid crosswise on marshy roads to make them firmer.

It is very hard for us to imagine how poor the early colonial roads were. In rainy weather, coaches and wagons sometimes sank up to their axles in mud. They cut deep ruts in the soft, wet ground. After the ground dried, these ruts made the roads very rough.

In marshy places, logs were sometimes laid crosswise along the roads to make them more firm. These log roads were called corduroy* roads. Passengers in stagecoaches that traveled on these bumpy corduroy roads were shaken so much that they could hardly talk to each other. A stagecoach that could travel ten miles a day over such poor roads was making good speed.

The first trail that led from the colonies into the unsettled land beyond the Appalachian Mountains* was called the Wilderness Road. Daniel Boone blazed this trail from Virginia into the heart of Kentucky in 1775. He cut gashes in the trunks of trees to show the way. His companions cut away small trees and underbrush to make a path through the forest. This path was wide enough for horses, but not for wagons. During the next few years, thousands of men, women, and children walked or rode on horseback over the Wilderness Road to the frontier.

After the Revolutionary War,* when Americans began moving westward in greater numbers, new roads were built to connect the East and West. Some of the new roads were built by private companies. These were called toll* roads, because the owners collected

The Wilderness Road led westward from Virginia into Kentucky. Daniel Boone blazed this trail in 1775.

The Lancaster Turnpike in Pennsylvania was America's first hard-surfaced toll* road.

money from travelers who used them. Some individuals and companies also built toll bridges.

America's first hard-surfaced toll road was opened in Pennsylvania in 1794. This sixty-two-mile road from Philadelphia to Lancaster was covered with hard-packed gravel. At each toll gate, the
traveler's way was blocked by a long pole across the road. On the
pole were sharp points called "pikes." When the travelers paid the
toll, the piked pole was turned aside so that they could pass. Because poles such as this were called "turnpikes," the road was

nicknamed the "Lancaster Turnpike." Some toll roads are still called turnpikes. (See map on page 52.)

In 1806 the United States Congress voted to build a national highway to the West. It was named the Cumberland Road, but later it became known as the National Road. The eastern part of this road was built with a center strip of crushed stone covered with gravel. From Cumberland, Maryland, to Wheeling, in what is now West Virginia, the road was eighty feet wide. The National Road was gradually extended westward, and by 1840 it had reached Vandalia, Illinois.

A toll house. People who owned private roads collected money from travelers who used these roads.

The National Road became the main route between the Atlantic coast and Ohio. For many years a steady stream of settlers followed this road as they traveled westward on foot, on horseback, and in covered wagons. Herds of cattle and hogs being driven east to market also crowded the busy highway. Racing past the slow-moving wagons and animals were the mail coaches. These sped from Cumberland to Wheeling in twenty-four hours. Today, part of U. S. Highway 40 follows almost the same route as that of the old National Road.

Pioneers on the National Road. A steady stream of settlers traveled westward on this road.

Traveling by stagecoach. Stagecoach lines carried passengers in America for more than 150 years.

5 The Stagecoach

What an adventure it was to travel from Boston to New York City in a stagecoach soon after the Revolutionary War!* At three o'clock in the morning you boarded a coach in Boston, and your journey began. Hour after hour, you bounced up and down on the hard wooden benches. The stagecoach had no springs, and the roads were very rough. Every fifteen or twenty miles you stopped while a fresh team of horses was hitched to the coach. Once, the wheels got stuck in a deep mudhole. With a sigh, you climbed out

31

The "Flying Machine" was a stage wagon drawn by four horses. It was named for its great speed.

into the mud with the other passengers and helped to push the coach free. About ten o'clock at night the driver stopped at an inn beside the road. You and the other tired passengers slept there for a few hours. Early in the morning you were up and ready to continue the six-day trip to New York.

Stagecoaches carried travelers from town to town in America for more than 150 years. America's first stagecoach lines were started in the early part of the eighteenth century. After the Revolutionary War, better roads were built. Then even more people traveled by stagecoach.

Early stagecoaches looked much like wagons. On each side of the coach were four slender poles which supported a light roof. Large leather curtains were attached to the roof at the back and on both sides. These curtains were lowered during rainstorms or snowstorms. Inside the stagecoach were four wooden benches. The driver and one or two passengers sat on the front bench. Nine passengers could sit on the other three benches. There were no doors, so the travelers had to climb in and out over the driver's bench. These coaches were often called "stage wagons."

Stagecoach passengers traveled more comfortably after the stage lines began using Concord coaches. The first of these was built in Concord, New Hampshire, about 1827. The body of a Concord coach was suspended on leather straps that served as

Stagecoach passengers on long journeys made overnight stops at inns along the way.

springs. Passengers in these coaches were not bounced and shaken so much as travelers in the earlier stage wagons were. Nine passengers could ride on the leather-upholstered seats inside a Concord coach, and more passengers could ride on the roof. The driver sat on the driver's box across the front of the coach. A Concord coach pulled by six horses could travel ten miles an hour on a good road.

In 1858 many travelers began to travel by stagecoach across the vast, unsettled territory between Missouri and California. This new stage line carried mail, supplies, and passengers to the rapidly growing cities on the west coast.

A Concord coach had room inside for nine passengers. More passengers could ride on the roof.

A western stagecoach did not stop at night. Passengers had to sleep sitting up as they rode.

To reach California, the western stagecoaches had to travel across plains, mountains, and deserts for twenty to twenty-five days. They were sometimes attacked by robbers or Indians along the way. Passengers had to sleep sitting up as they rode over the rough trail, for these coaches did not stop at night. By the latter part of the 1800's, stagecoaches had been replaced by railroads in many parts of the West.

A wagon train moving westward. Each covered wagon was a home on wheels for a pioneer family.

6 Covered Wagons

A long line of covered wagons moves slowly westward across the Nebraska prairies. All of them have large, white canvas tops that billow in the wind. They make the wagons look so much like sailing ships that people have nicknamed them "prairie schooners." Each wagon is a home on wheels for a pioneer family making the long trip to Oregon. All of the family's possessions are packed inside their covered wagon.

As sunset nears, the wagon master signals that the day's march is over. Earlier in the day, one of the men rode ahead of the wagon train to find this camping place. It is near a stream of fresh, clear water. The wagons park so that they form a big circle. Inside the circle, campfires are lighted and women cook the evening meal. After supper, people gather around the fires. They sing and tell stories. Some men stay outside the circle of wagons to guard the horses and cattle. They also watch for Indians who might attack the wagon train in the night.

Hitching oxen to wagons in the morning. By about seven o'clock, the wagons were ready to move.

At four o'clock the next morning the guards fire their rifles. This is the signal for everyone to get up. Breakfast is eaten, and the oxen are hitched to the wagons. About seven o'clock the drivers crack their whips, and the prairie schooners again move slowly across the prairies.

These pioneer families met at Independence, Missouri, in the spring to form their wagon train. They began their journey in spring so that there would be grass growing along the route for their cattle and horses to eat. If they are lucky, the wagon train will complete the two-thousand-mile trip to Oregon in five months.

The journey westward was started in spring so the oxen would have grass to eat along the way.

Crossing a river. Pioneers sometimes built rafts to float covered wagons across deep streams.

Long before pioneers crossed the plains in prairie schooners, covered wagons were driven along the roads and turnpikes in the eastern part of America. Most of these were Conestoga wagons. They were given this name because the first ones were built at Conestoga, Pennsylvania.

Conestogas were well suited for hauling heavy loads over poor roads. These huge covered wagons were usually pulled by four or six horses. They could haul loads weighing as much as six tons.

Crossing a bridge. Covered wagons called "Conestogas" were used for hauling freight in the East.

The wheels of a Conestoga were broad so that they would not easily sink in a muddy road. The wagon's body was watertight. It could be floated across a stream where there was no bridge. To prevent goods from sliding back and forth, the floor curved upward at each end. A white canvas cover was stretched across the top of the wagon. This protected goods inside from snow or rain. The underbody of a Conestoga was painted blue, and the wooden sideboards were painted bright red. Often the horses' harnesses were trimmed in red and decorated with bells.

Many kinds of freight were carried in Conestogas. Merchants and manufacturers shipped goods from town to town in these huge wagons. Farmers used them to haul their produce to market. Many pioneer families traveled in them across the Allegheny Mountains* to the new frontier. In the West, traders traveling

A Conestoga wagon could carry up to six tons of freight. It was pulled by horses or oxen.

along the Santa Fe Trail* carried blankets, cloth, silk, and other goods in Conestogas.

Tens of thousands of covered wagons moved slowly along the roads of America during the last half of the eighteenth century and much of the nineteenth century.

Preparing to travel westward on the Santa Fe Trail.* This trail began in Independence, Missouri.

A flatboat. After the Revolutionary War,* many pioneer families traveled west in flatboats.

7 Flatboats on the Rivers

After the Revolutionary War,* thousands of pioneer families traveled west in flatboats. In 1787 the government opened the land west of the Appalachian Mountains* and north of the Ohio River for settlement. There were few roads west of the mountains, and most pioneers traveled by boat into this region. They used several kinds of boats, but the flatboat was most commonly used.

43

Steering a flatboat down the Ohio. Pioneer families sometimes lived on flatboats for several weeks.

Pioneer families built flatboats or bought them at towns along the upper Ohio River. Many of these families came from the east coast in wagons or on horseback. They knew nothing about boat travel on the Ohio. Sometimes they hired a boatman to go down the river with them. A skillful boatman could guide a flatboat from Pittsburgh to Cincinnati in about a week.

The flatboats were of different sizes. Some were only about twenty feet long and ten feet wide. The larger boats were about sixty feet long and twenty feet wide. A flatboat looked much like a big floating box. It was steered with a long oar, called a sweep. The sweep was usually about as long as the boat.

Flatboats were like floating homes for the pioneers. Families sometimes lived on them for several weeks as they drifted slowly downstream. They spent much of their time on the roof of the boat. Sometimes the father played his fiddle while the children danced on the roof.

Jolly boatmen. People on flatboats sometimes danced or played cards to pass the time.

Usually several flatboats traveled together so that families could help each other in times of trouble. Sometimes flatboats were attacked by Indians. There were also river pirates who fired on the boats. If a boat got caught on a sand bar or a sunken log, the pioneers might have to work for several days to free it.

People who settled along the Ohio and Mississippi rivers shipped their farm products to market in flatboats. Boats loaded with grain, flour, tobacco, and furs drifted downstream to New

An attack on a flatboat. Indians or river pirates sometimes attacked the pioneers.

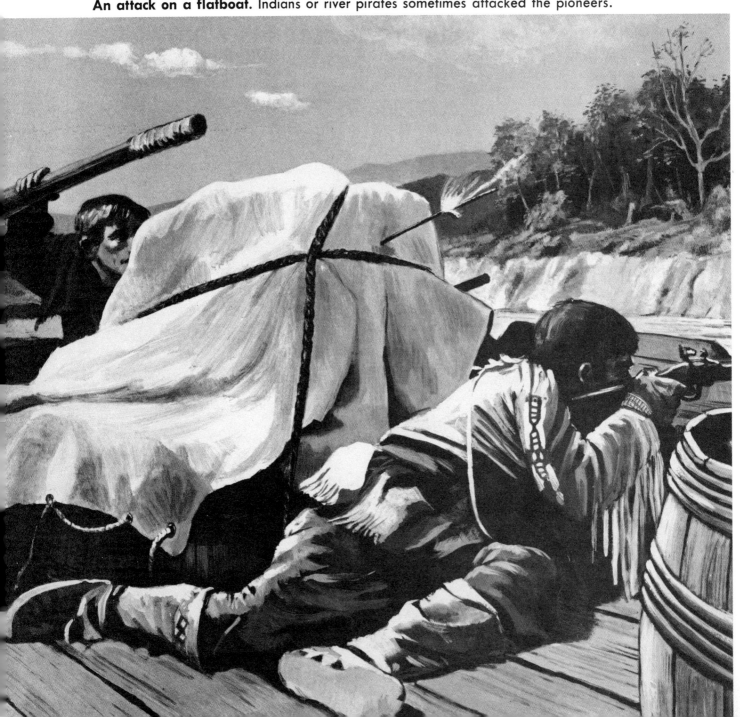

A flatboat carried freight downstream. At the journey's end, the boat was sold for lumber.

Orleans. At the end of the trip, the flatboats were taken apart and sold as lumber, for it was too difficult to pole them back upstream.

The slow-moving flatboats were gradually replaced by steam-boats. These could travel faster and could go upstream as well as downstream. By 1860 there were almost no flatboats on the rivers.

The Erie Canal. Passenger boats and barges used this waterway in New York State.

8 Canalboat Days

It is a bright summer day in 1835—a perfect day for a trip on the Erie Canal.* Let's board the "Whirlwind," a gaily painted packet* boat. Two large horses are hitched to a towline that is fastened to the boat. As they walk along the towpath beside the canal, they pull the boat slowly through the water. We decide to sit with the other passengers on the flat roof of the cabin. Suddenly a man yells, "Everybody down!" We duck our heads as the boat glides under a low bridge. When the boat passes near the shore, we jump onto the towpath for a short walk along the grassy canal bank.

We climb back on board in time for supper, which is served in the main cabin. Later in the evening, the women go to their room, and the dining room is converted into a dormitory* for the men. Twenty-one berths are arranged on each side of this room. However, there are forty-eight men passengers. Late-comers have to sleep on the dining tables.

Horses towing a boat along the Erie Canal. This canal was forty feet wide and four feet deep.

Canal locks were used to raise or lower boats from one waterway to another.

Next morning, as we sit on the sunny cabin roof, we wave to the passengers of a line boat moving slowly down the canal. Many of the people on the line boat are pioneers moving west. They cannot afford to ride on the faster and more comfortable packet boats. On the line boats passengers furnish their own food and bedding. The passengers say, "Traveling on a line boat is a cent and a half a mile, a mile and a half an hour."

Soon we pass a wide, flat, freight barge loaded with sacks of grain and kegs of whiskey. We see other barges carrying loads of timber and furs. Before the Erie Canal was completed it cost one

50

hundred dollars to ship a ton of freight overland from Buffalo to New York City. The trip took at least twenty days. The barges we see are carrying freight the same distance in eight days for only five to ten dollars a ton.

People in America have always used their country's waterways for cheap, convenient transportation. Before canals were built, however, river travel was often difficult. If there were waterfalls or rapids in a river, the cargo had to be taken off the boat, hauled around the rapids, and then reloaded on another boat.

To make it possible for boats to travel farther without being unloaded, short canals were dug around some of the rapids and waterfalls. The first was a seven-mile-long canal built in Virginia in 1785. Boats traveled through this waterway around falls in the James River.* Many such canals were soon built in other states.

Canals were also built to connect one waterway with another. Before the year 1825 there was no water highway on which boats could travel between the Great Lakes and the rivers in the eastern part of the United States. Because it was very expensive to haul freight overland, people wanted to build a canal to connect these two parts of the country.

In 1817 the state of New York began building the Erie Canal to link New York City with the Midwest. This huge ditch reached 363 miles, from Buffalo to the Hudson River. (See map on page 52.) It was forty feet wide at the surface, twenty-eight feet wide at the bottom, and four feet deep. When the Erie Canal was completed, in 1825, boats could travel from Lake Erie to the Hudson River, and down that river to New York City. Soon large amounts of raw materials and manufactured goods were being transported on this water highway. This trade aided the growth of New York

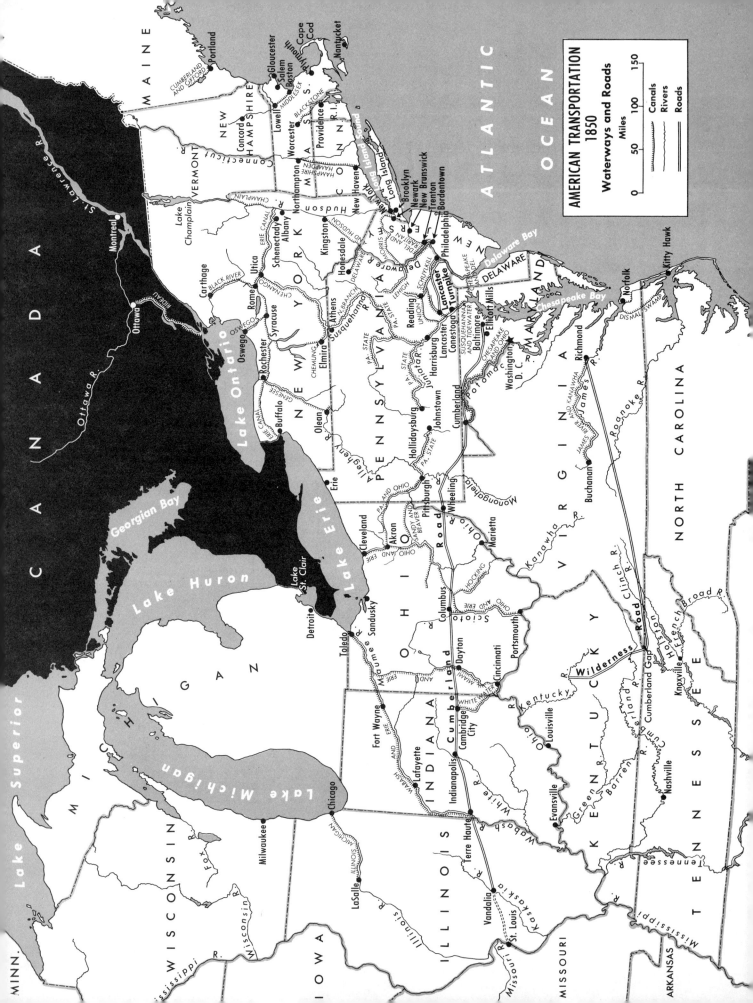

AMERICAN TRANSPORTATION 1850
Waterways and Roads

Canals ....
Rivers ∿∿∿∿
Roads ━━━━

Miles

0   50   100   150

American waterways and roads in 1850. A network of canals linked the rivers of the interior with the Great Lakes and the Atlantic Ocean.

and other cities along the route. In the early 1900's the Erie Canal became part of a great system of canals in New York State.

After the Erie Canal was finished, other canals were built to carry coal from the mines of eastern Pennsylvania to Atlantic ports. Hundreds of miles of canals joined the rivers of the Midwest with the Great Lakes. (See map on opposite page.) By 1833, canals made it possible for people to travel by boat from New York City to the Ohio River.

In the 1850's railroads replaced canals in many parts of our country. (Chapters 13 and 14 tell about the development of railroads in the United States.) However, canals are still important in some places. For example, many ships today use the Soo Canals that connect Lake Superior with the other Great Lakes.

Traveling on the Soo Canal. This canal connects Lake Superior with the other Great Lakes.

A wharf* in New York. In the 1800's, sailing ships from all over the world docked at New York.

9 Sailing Ships

We are visiting the harbor of New York City on a fine summer day in 1840. Anchored along the wharf* are many sailing ships. Some are large and some are small. Looking across the harbor, we see row upon row of tall masts pointing to the sky. Nearby, the last supplies are being loaded on a packet* liner. This large ship makes regular trips to Europe. As travelers board the packet liner, their friends wave to them from the pier. We stroll down the

Sailing ships in New York Harbor in 1850. American sailing vessels carried freight and passengers to and from Europe and the Orient.*

Trading vessels at anchor in a Chinese harbor. American trade with China began in 1784.

wharf and stop beside a trading ship that has just returned from the Orient.* Workers are carrying bales of Indian cotton and bags of coffee from this ship. If we were to visit any other seaport on the northeastern coast of America at this time, we would see the same busy scene.

American sea captains began sailing ships to China soon after the Revolutionary War.* The first ship to make this trip was the "Empress of China." Soon after this ship sailed, in 1784, many other ships began traveling to and from the Orient.

Most of the China traders sailed from Boston or Salem, Massachusetts. The captains from Boston sailed their ships around South America to the western coast of North America. There they stopped to load their ships with furs. Then they sailed on across the Pacific to trade these furs in China. Ships from Salem sailed across the Atlantic and around the southern tip of Africa to reach China. Along the way they picked up goods to trade in India and China.

The first trading vessels that sailed to China were small. Most of them were only sixty-five to ninety feet long. These small ships were best for sailing into the shallow inlets on the western coast of America. They could pass over sand bars that might wreck a larger ship. These ships carried large crews and many guns. The people in the lands they visited were not always friendly. Sometimes the sailors had to fight.

China traders did not make fast trips. They sailed slowly from one port to another, picking up goods to trade in the Orient. When they returned to America, these ships brought cargoes of tea, silk, tableware, Indian cotton goods, spices, and other Oriental products.

American ships began sailing regularly between Europe and America in 1816. In that year, a packet line between New York and Liverpool, England, was started. A packet liner was a ship that sailed between two ports on a regular schedule. It carried both passengers and freight. Ships on the first packet line sailed once each month from New York. By 1830, packets were sailing to London twice a month and to France three times a month. Packet liners were also sailing to South America and Mexico.

American packet ships were bigger, faster, and safer than most of the sailing vessels of that time. They usually sailed to England in about twenty days. The trip back to New York took longer, because the winds usually blew toward the east. Although there were only about fifty ships in the American packet lines, they carried much of the passenger and freight trade of the Atlantic Ocean.

A **packet*** **liner** carried both passengers and freight. A trip to England took about twenty days.

An American clipper ship in Hong Kong harbor. Clipper ships were the fastest ships on the sea.

10 Clipper Ships and Schooners

Halfway around the world in three months! People in London, England, in 1850, could hardly believe the news. They hurried to the London docks to see the amazing American ship that had sailed from China to England in only ninety-one days. This was the "Oriental," the first clipper ship to dock at London.

59

A clipper was a slim, graceful ship that carried a great cloud of white canvas sails. The tallest of its three masts usually reached two hundred feet above the water. A group of huge sails stretched to the top of each mast. The clipper's wooden hull was long and slender, with a sharply pointed bow. It was usually painted black. The contrast between the black hull and the great, billowing

A clipper had three masts and huge white sails. Its slender hull was usually painted black.

white sails added to the beauty of the clipper as it cut swiftly through the water.

The famous clipper ships of the 1840's and the 1850's were patterned after a ship designed by John Griffiths.* This ship, named the "Rainbow," was launched in 1845. The "Rainbow's" sails were so high and the hull was so narrow that many sailors thought it would overturn. However, it could sail to China faster than any other ship. Soon many American shipyards began building vessels similar to the "Rainbow." By 1853, two hundred and seventy clippers had been built. The most famous builder of this type of ship was Donald McKay.* He built the "Great Republic," the largest of the clippers. The deck of this ship was 325 feet long.

During the Gold Rush,* thousands of people sailed on clipper ships to California. Before the time of clippers it took 180 days to sail from New York to San Francisco. Clippers could make the voyage in eighty-nine days. A trip on one of these fast ships took less time than traveling overland by wagon.

America's clipper ships traveled all over the world. They were used for carrying freight from the Orient.* Cargoes of tea and spices had to be transported quickly so they would not lose their freshness. Merchants shipped such cargoes on fast-sailing American clippers.

Clippers were the fastest ships on the sea for only a short time, however. During the 1850's, English shipbuilders began to build iron steamships that were faster than the clippers. By 1860, steamships carried many of the cargoes once transported by clippers.

Soon after American shipyards began building clipper ships, they also began to build large, three-masted schooners. Schooners had been used in this country since 1713, but they were small and

61

Donald McKay* watching one of his clippers. He was the most famous builder of this type of ship.

had only two masts. By 1873, many three-masted schooners were carrying freight along the American coasts. These ships transported freight more cheaply than other sailing ships because they were operated by small crews.

It was not long until larger schooners were launched. Schooners with four, five, or six masts were being used by 1900. A seven-masted schooner, the largest of them all, was built in 1902.

Schooners were used for shipping bulky cargoes, such as coal, stone, cotton, or sugar along the east coast. They were also used to ship lumber along the west coast. Although sailing ships were gradually replaced by steamships, schooners continued to carry freight for many years.

A seven-masted schooner. This ship, built in 1902, was the largest schooner ever built.

The "Clermont" was the world's first successful steamboat. It was designed by Robert Fulton.*

11 The First Steamboats

On August 17, 1807, a large crowd of people gathered at a Hudson River* wharf in New York City. They were watching a strange, new boat called the "Clermont," which was ready for its first trip on the water. Many people in the crowd thought that the boat would not run. It was designed by Robert Fulton,* and the people had nicknamed it "Fulton's Folly."

Clouds of black smoke poured from the tall, thirty-foot smoke-stack. Suddenly the big paddle wheels on either side of the boat began churning the water, and the boat moved slowly away from the dock. The people cheered as it went steadily up the Hudson River. This was the world's first successful steamboat.

The "Clermont" continued up the river, driven entirely by steam power. Excited people gathered on the riverbanks along the way to watch the boat. As it steamed on, smoke poured from the smokestack, and the engine made loud, clanking noises. Some fishermen were so frightened by the "Clermont" that they jumped into the water. Others quickly rowed their boats to the shore. The steamboat seemed like a monster to these men. It was the first ship driven entirely by steam that they had ever seen.

America's first steamboat. In 1786 John Fitch* built the first steamboat in America.

The "Clermont" was not the first steamboat. In making it, Robert Fulton borrowed successful ideas from earlier experiments of other men. One of these early inventors was John Fitch,* who had built the first steamboat in America in 1786. The boat that Fitch designed had six paddles on each side. These were operated

An early steamboat built by John Fitch. None of Fitch's steamboats were completely successful.

The Brooklyn ferry traveled between New York City and Brooklyn. Many ferries used steam power.

by steam power. They moved the boat through the water at about three miles an hour. Fitch built several other steamboats. One of these made regular trips on the Delaware River in 1790. However, its engine was not powerful enough to move the boat when it was heavily loaded. Several other Americans had also built steamboats, but none were completely successful.

67

Steamboats on the Hudson River. * Many steamboats were built after the success of the "Clermont."

The "Clermont" was called the first successful steamboat because it was the first one to carry passengers regularly and to operate at a profit. Two weeks after its first voyage, this ship began making regular trips up and down the Hudson River.

After the success of the "Clermont," many other steamboats were built to carry travelers up and down the rivers of America.

Fulton built several more steamboats for travel on the Hudson
River. Travelers crowded each new boat that was added to the
steamboat line. By 1827, there were many steamboats on the
Hudson and on other rivers of the United States.

A cabin of a river steamer. Some Hudson River steamboats had large, comfortable staterooms.

A steamboat on the Mississippi. River steamers had flat-bottomed hulls and double decks.

12 River Steamers

By the middle of the nineteenth century, Americans were traveling on river steamboats that seemed like "fairy palaces" to many of the passengers. The wooden railings and roofs were carved in lacy designs, which were painted white and trimmed with gold. Pictures were painted on the stateroom doors and on the huge boxes that enclosed the paddle wheels of the boat. Large cut-glass chandeliers* hung from the ceilings of some rooms, and thick carpets covered the floors. Many steamers hired brass bands or orchestras to entertain the passengers. Rich, tasty food was served in the dining rooms. Americans could travel very comfortably on these elaborate river steamers.

The "New Orleans" was the first steamboat on a river west of the Appalachian Mountains.* It sailed down the Ohio and Mississippi rivers in 1811. By 1814, three more steamers had been launched on the Ohio River. However, none of the early steamers could sail upstream on these two rivers, for they had very strong currents. The flow of the currents against the deep, dragging hulls of these boats prevented them from moving upstream.

In 1816 Henry Shreve* built a steamboat designed especially for use on the Mississippi. The hull of this boat was nearly flat,

The lounge of a river steamer seemed like a fairy palace to many of the passengers.

and the engine was placed on the main deck instead of in the hull. An upper deck was added for additional space. This boat, which was named the "Washington," traveled upstream on the Mississippi and Ohio rivers in 1817. After this successful trip, Shreve's boat became a model for all river steamboats. Many more flat-bottomed, double-decked steamers were soon built. Within a few years, steamboats were turning the western rivers of America into busy water highways.

By 1846, the river steamers were carrying more freight than all the oceangoing ships that sailed between the United States and other lands. The boats also carried many passengers from one river town to another. Night and day the giant paddle wheels churned the water as the boats steamed up and down the Ohio, Mississippi, and Missouri rivers.

Stern-wheelers had one large paddle wheel at the rear, instead of one on each side.

A river steamer. Steamboats carried cargoes along the Ohio, Mississippi, and Missouri rivers.

Steamboats carried most of the freight that was shipped to and from towns along the rivers. Meat, cast-iron products, barrels, and cloth were put on the steamers at Pittsburgh, Cincinnati, and Louisville. At towns on the Missouri River and along the upper Mississippi, the boats were loaded with furs, skins, farm products, and lead. Along the lower Mississippi, the steamers picked up sugar and cotton. Most of this river freight was carried downstream to New Orleans. There it was shipped to the eastern part of the United States or to other countries. However, sugar, coffee, and heavy machinery were shipped up the river.

Steamboat captains were continually trying to set new speed records. The trip from New Orleans to Louisville took twenty-five

73

A steamboat race. River steamers often raced each other from one river town to another.

days in 1817. By 1853, however, the record time for this distance was less than four and one-half days. Steamboats often raced against each other from one river town to another. Hundreds of people gathered on the riverbanks to watch these exciting races. The people cheered as their favorite boat steamed by, and they waited anxiously to hear which steamer won the race. Sometimes a captain tried to drive his steamboat so fast that the boiler exploded and people were killed.

In 1860, steamboats on the western rivers carried more passengers and freight than ever before. There were about two thousand steamers on the rivers at that time. In 1861, however, many boats stopped operating because of the war which started between the North and the South. By the time the war ended, in 1865, railroads were carrying much of the freight once transported by steamboats.

Unloading cargo. By 1865, railroads were carrying much of the freight once carried by steamboats.

The "DeWitt Clinton" was one of the earliest steam locomotives built in America.

13 The Coming of the Railroad

On August 9, 1831, a large crowd of people gathered in the city of Albany, New York. They stared curiously at a little steam engine about twelve feet long. This was the "DeWitt Clinton," one of the first steam locomotives in America. Passengers had filled every seat in the coaches. Even the benches on the small flatcars behind the coaches were crowded with people. Suddenly great clouds of black smoke began to billow from the smokestack, and the little engine jerked into motion. The startled passengers were jolted off their seats as the train started down the track.

Showers of burning sparks poured from the tall smokestack. Several passengers shouted as sparks from the engine burned holes in their clothes. People on the flatcars put umbrellas over their heads to keep off the burning sparks. Soon the umbrellas began to smolder, too. Startled crows flew up from cornfields as the passengers threw their burning umbrellas off the train. Before long, the seventeen-mile trip to Schenectady* was over. The tired, sooty passengers were amazed when the engineer told them how fast they had traveled. The little "DeWitt Clinton" had reached a speed of thirty miles an hour!

An early railroad car. The first railroad cars in America were pulled by horses.

The first American railroad built to carry passengers and freight was the Baltimore and Ohio. Horse-drawn trains began running on its thirteen-mile track from Baltimore to Ellicott Mills, Maryland, in 1830. The fare for one way was nine cents. Soon travelers could also ride on trains in South Carolina, New York, Pennsylvania, New Jersey, and Massachusetts. Most of these railroads were short. They usually connected only two cities.

Early railroad companies experimented with several kinds of power for their trains. Horses pulled the first railroad cars. Some railroad companies tried sailcars. These looked much like sailboats on wheels. Sailcars were not successful, however, because they could travel only when there was a good wind. Steam locomotives

A sailcar. Some of the early railroad companies experimented with wind power.

A famous race. In 1830, the locomotive "Tom Thumb" raced a horse-drawn car. The horse won.

were also given trial runs on the early railroads. Most companies soon decided to use locomotives to pull their trains.

One of the first American steam locomotives was called the "Tom Thumb," because it was so small. In 1830 the "Tom Thumb" made a trial run on the thirteen-mile track of the Baltimore and Ohio. The little locomotive pulled a car carrying thirty-six passengers over the track in less than an hour. Soon after this trip, the "Tom Thumb" was challenged to race a horse-drawn railroad car.

79

An early train. Passengers could ride inside or on the roofs of some early railroad coaches.

The horse led at the start, but within a few miles the "Tom Thumb" pulled out in front. The locomotive continued to lead until engine trouble caused it to lose speed. Then the horse passed the little engine and won the race. ·

When the first railroads were built in America, many people were opposed to them. Some said trains were too dangerous. Others said that it was sinful to go so fast. Farmers complained that the locomotives made so much noise that hens stopped laying eggs. The protests were soon forgotten, however, and people became enthusiastic about railroad travel.

80

Travelers on the first trains actually rode in stagecoaches. The wheels of the stagecoaches had been replaced with flanged* wheels so that the coaches could run on rails. Soon, however, a new type of passenger car was being used.

The new railroad coach was long and boxlike, with a door at each end. A narrow aisle ran down the center of the car. Wooden benches were placed crosswise on either side of the aisle. In the winter, the coach was heated by a huge, wood-burning stove at one end of the car. The passengers who sat near the stove were usually perspiring. Those at the other end of the coach often shivered from the cold.

Passengers board a train. Many Americans were eager to ride on early railroad trains.

Although railroad travel was uncomfortable, many Americans were eager to ride on trains. They could travel faster and more comfortably by train than by the other means of land transportation then in use. By 1860, there were more than thirty thousand miles of railroad tracks in the United States.

An American express train. Travel by rail was faster than any other kind of land travel.

Building the first coast-to-coast railroad. On May 10, 1869, this railroad was completed.

14 Railroads Unite the Nation

The first railroad to connect California with the eastern part of the country was built by two railroad companies which were racing to see which one could lay the most track. Congress had voted to give the companies ten square miles of land along the railroad for every mile of track laid. Each company wanted to lay more track so that it would receive the most land.

Congress had made plans to build this railroad in 1862. Thousands of people had moved west to build new homes in Oregon, or to seek gold in California. There was no way to travel quickly between these areas and the eastern part of the United States. The railroad at that time reached only as far west as Missouri. From there, travelers went by stagecoach or by wagon to the west coast. The stagecoach trip took about twenty-five days, and the wagon trip nearly five months.

The two companies which Congress chartered* to build the railroad were the Central Pacific and the Union Pacific. The Central Pacific started laying track eastward from Sacramento,

Chasing buffalo. Large buffalo herds sometimes blocked the railroad tracks on the Great Plains.

Traveling west. Many people began to move westward by train as well as by covered wagon.

California in 1864. It brought in thousands of workers from China to do this work. The next year, the Union Pacific began laying track westward from Omaha, Nebraska. Many of its workers were people who had recently come to the United States from Europe.

Both companies faced great difficulties as they raced toward each other. The builders of the Central Pacific had to lay their tracks across the rugged Sierra Nevada.* There was no easy pass through these mountains, and many bridges and tunnels had to be built. All the supplies had to be shipped by boat from the east coast to California. The Union Pacific brought supplies up the Missouri River by boat and then overland by wagon. The route they followed lay across land inhabited by Indians. These people did not like the

Families journeying to new homes in the West. Railroad trains were faster than wagon trains.

railroad crossing their land. Sometimes half the railroad workers had to fight Indians while the others laid the track.

On May 10, 1869, the tracks met at Promontory, Utah. As hundreds of people watched, officials of the two companies drove a gold spike into the final railroad tie. The news was telegraphed across the nation. Bells chimed and cannons boomed in many cities to celebrate the completion of the railroad. The Union Pacific had laid 1,086 miles of the new track, and the Central Pacific had laid 689 miles.

A train in the mountains. In rugged regions, two locomotives were often needed to pull the railroad cars up steep slopes.

The transcontinental* railroad made it possible for Americans to travel more quickly and easily. Many people who wished to settle in the West now traveled by train to their new homes. This was not only faster but also much safer than crossing the plains in a covered wagon. By 1870, a train trip from coast to coast took only six days.

Trade between the East and the West increased as more western railroads were built. Trains carried manufactured goods from the East to towns and cities in the West. On the return trip to eastern cities, the trains were loaded with produce from western farms and cattle from western ranges.

Railroad yards in 1877. Trade between East and West grew as more western railroads were built.

The Pennsylvania Railroad and several other railroad companies could not make enough money to stay in business. They were joined together to form a new company called Conrail.

The railroads that crossed our vast country helped to unite us into one mighty nation. For many years, railroads were the most important way of traveling and transporting goods. Then automobiles, trucks, and airplanes came into use. By the 1950's, these newer forms of transportation had taken away much of the railroads' business.

Since then, railroad companies have worked hard to encourage people to ship goods by rail. Different kinds of railroad cars have been built to carry different products. For example, tank cars have been built to carry chemicals. Refrigerated cars have been built to carry vegetables and frozen foods. Special railroad cars have been designed to carry automobiles stacked one above the other. Trucks loaded with goods are also carried piggyback on railroad cars.

When they reach their destination, these trucks are driven off and take their goods to where they are needed.

The United States government has also worked to help rail transportation. In the 1970's, it helped to form a company called Conrail. Conrail took over the equipment and railroad tracks of seven companies in the northeastern part of the country that could not make enough money to stay in business. It received money from the government to keep the freight trains running.

To keep passenger trains running, the government helped form another company called Amtrak. Like Conrail, it receives money to keep the trains running. Almost all the passenger trains in the United States are owned by Amtrak. Amtrak trains travel to over 500 cities and towns. They have comfortable, air-conditioned coaches. Many people are enjoying the convenience of traveling in Amtrak trains.

A passenger train. In the 1970's Amtrak took over almost all the passenger trains.

A New York street in 1819. Most people rode in carriages, or walked, before omnibuses were used.

15 Transportation in the City

What a noisy, uncomfortable experience it was to ride through the streets of New York City in an omnibus. Imagine that you are standing with a crowd of people on a street corner in 1835. You are waiting to board one of these horse-drawn buses. Now you can see the omnibus coming toward you down the rough cobblestone street. It looks like a huge box on wheels. The driver, sitting on the roof of the bus, pulls at the horses' reins, and the bus lurches to a stop near the corner. A door at the back opens, and you crowd in with the other passengers. You pay your fare by dropping twelve and one-half cents into a fare

Omnibuses in New York. By 1855, there were hundreds of omnibuses in the larger American cities.

box, which the driver has lowered through the roof. One man shouts up at the driver through the hole in the roof, because he has received no change. Other passengers push and shove you as you try to find an empty seat on one of the wooden benches.

Now the horses are running at full speed. A man in the front seat shouts up to the driver, "Slow down!" Two children begin to cry. The boy in the seat beside you leans out of the window and yells at the horses to go faster. The man in the front seat stands up to shout at the driver again and is bumped roughly back in his seat as the bus jolts along.

The driver pays no attention to all this noise and confusion. In fact, he can hardly hear it. His signal to stop finally comes when the elderly man across from you pulls a strap that runs along the top of the bus and through the hole in the roof. This strap is attached to the driver's leg. When he feels the tug on the strap, he stops the bus. As soon as the back door opens, you and the elderly man get off. You have decided to walk the rest of the way home.

The first American omnibus was built in New York City in 1829. It looked somewhat like a large stagecoach. Later on, the buses were boxlike in shape. By 1855, there were hundreds of omnibuses in the cities of Philadelphia, Boston, and Baltimore, as well as New York. Until street railways were started, omnibuses were the chief means of transportation for people in the cities.

New York in 1876. For many years, omnibuses were the chief means of transportation in cities.

Railway tracks were laid in the streets of several American cities in the 1860's. Large streetcars were pulled over the rails by two horses. Smaller cars, called "bobtails," were pulled by one horse. These cars were about twelve feet long and had seats for eighteen passengers. Some of the first streetcars had steps leading to the roof, where there were seats for more passengers. The cars were not heated in winter, but straw was thrown on the floors to help keep the passengers' feet warm.

A "bobtail" streetcar was pulled on rails by one horse. It had seats for eighteen passengers.

An electric trolley car ran on rails. It was powered by electricity from an overhead cable.

Late in the nineteenth century, horse-drawn streetcars were replaced by trolley cars in many cities. Trolley cars also ran on rails. They were often called electric streetcars. A long metal pole extended from the top of a trolley car to an overhead cable. Electric power traveled through this pole from the cable to the motor in the car. The early trolley cars could go about twelve miles an hour.

95

A railroad was built above the streets of New York City in 1867. Small steam locomotives pulled passenger cars along the tracks of this elevated railway. Many people in the city did not want these noisy trains rushing overhead. By 1876, however, forty trains a day were running on the elevated railroad. The fare was

An elevated railway. The first elevated trains were powered by steam. Later, electricity was used.

A subway. America's first underground electric railroad was opened in Boston in 1898.

five cents during rush hours, and ten cents at other times. Elevated railroads were also built in Brooklyn, Chicago, and Boston. By 1901, most elevated trains were powered by electricity.

As their streets became more and more crowded, some cities began to build underground railroads. These were called subways. America's first subway was opened in Boston in 1898. Construction was started on a New York subway two years later. Swift electric subway trains still operate in several cities in the United States. They carry thousands of passengers daily.

The first city motorbuses were put into use in the early 1900's. As time went on, buses replaced streetcars in most cities. Buses could move through traffic more easily than streetcars, because they did not have to run on rails.

Today, millions of people in large cities ride on buses and subways. However, many city people prefer to use cars. This has made it difficult for some bus companies to stay in business. It has also caused traffic and parking problems. City governments are working on solving these problems.

A city bus. The first motorbuses were put into use in the early 1900's.

Bicycling on a Sunday afternoon in 1895. These people are riding bicycles called "safeties."

16 The Bicycle

Imagine that you are visiting an American city on a Sunday afternoon ninety years ago. The streets are crowded with bicycle riders. Some of the cyclists are bicycle club members who are riding into the country on an all-day trip. You hear shouts of young people as they race ahead of their friends. You see families riding their bicycles together. Many of them carry lunch baskets as they cycle to the picnic grounds.

99

A "**hobbyhorse**" was a bicycle without pedals. The rider moved the bicycle forward by walking.

Bicycles were sold in America in the early part of the nineteenth century, but only a few people bought them. The first bicycle had no pedals. The rider's feet touched the ground as he perched on the seat, and he moved the bike forward by walking. This bicycle was invented in 1816. It was called a "hobbyhorse."

In the 1860's a bicycle called a "velocipede"* was made. It had pedals attached to the center of the front wheel. Rims of heavy iron were fastened to the wooden wheels. The frame was made of thick metal. These bicycles became known as "bone-shakers" because their riders were shaken so much as they pedaled over the rough streets.

The design of bicycles was changed again a few years later. The new bicycle was called an "ordinary." It could go much faster than a velocipede. The ordinary had a very large front wheel and a small back wheel. These wheels had wire spokes, steel rims, and rubber tires. The seat was located above the front wheel. On some of the largest ordinaries, the rider sat five feet above the ground. If you were going to ride one of these high machines, you would have to find something high to stand on in order to climb onto the seat. If you fell off, it would be difficult to get back on again. You might have to push your ordinary a long way before you found something high enough to stand on to climb onto the seat!

Velocipedes* were called "bone-shakers." Rims of heavy iron were fastened on their wooden wheels.

The ordinary was so dangerous and so difficult to mount that another type of bicycle was designed. This one was called a "safety." It looked much like the bicycles of today. By the year 1890, almost every cyclist rode a safety.

People enjoyed riding this new bicycle so much that bicycling clubs were organized in many towns and cities. Club members often spent their Sundays and holidays taking long rides in the country. One national club gave medals to cyclists who could do a "century." To do a century, the cyclist rode in any direction for

Members of a bicycle club riding "ordinaries." This type of bicycle was very dangerous.

A bicycle built for two. The tandem bicycle had two seats, two handlebars, and two sets of pedals.

fifty miles, then turned around and rode the fifty miles back. The round trip was expected to take no more than ten hours.

Today you may hear an old song about a "bicycle built for two," but you rarely see one of them. At the end of the nineteenth century, however, bicycles built for two were very popular. They were called tandem bicycles. A tandem had two seats, two handlebars, and two sets of pedals. Many couples enjoyed riding on tandem bicycles.

After 1900, fewer and fewer people used bicycles. Everyone was interested in a new machine called an automobile. Many bicycle manufacturers went out of business. During the 1930's, however, bicycles again became popular. Manufacturers made many improvements in them. Today, a cyclist can pedal uphill easily on a lightweight, ten-speed bicycle.

Car trouble at night. Drivers of early automobiles often had to make their own car repairs.

17 Automobiles

How exciting it is to bump along the road in a high, open-topped automobile! The sun is warm on this dry, summer day in 1904. The duster* and goggles you are wearing protect you from the clouds of powdery dust stirred up by your car. You brace your feet as the car jolts over rocks and ruts in the unpaved road. Suddenly one wheel slips into a rut, and the engine stops. You get out and turn the metal crank on the front to start the motor. You jump quickly into the driver's seat before the motor has a chance to stop again.

105

An early automobile. By the year 1900, there were about eight thousand automobiles in the United States.

A 1901 Oldsmobile. The first automobiles were called "horseless carriages."

Soon you pass a grassy meadow. Startled colts kick their heels high into the air and dash off across the field. A horse-drawn buggy pulls off the road. The driver holds his hat over the frightened horse's eyes as you chug by. When you drive into a small town, everybody scurries to the side of the street. People run to the doors of their houses to stare at your noisy "horseless carriage."

The first gasoline-driven automobile in America was built by the Duryea* brothers of Massachusetts in 1893. Inventors had already experimented with steam and electric automobiles, and people argued a great deal about which was the best kind of car.

106

Gradually, most people agreed that automobiles with gasoline engines were best. By the year 1900, there were eight thousand automobiles in the United States. However, they cost so much that most people could not afford to buy them. During the early 1900's, many people thought automobiles were "playthings of the rich."

The introduction of the "Tin Lizzie," in 1908, made it possible for many more Americans to own automobiles. Tin Lizzie was the nickname given to the Model T Ford, which was produced by Henry Ford.* The 1908 model could travel forty miles an hour. It could run twenty-two miles on a gallon of gasoline. Many families who had never owned a car were able to buy a Model T. These cars cost about eight hundred dollars. Within nine years

A Model T Ford was called a "Tin Lizzie." Many Americans were able to buy these inexpensive cars.

Horses pulling an automobile out of the mud. Better roads were needed for automobile travel.

the price had dropped to less than four hundred dollars, and millions of shiny, black Model T's were being sold.

Tin Lizzies were especially well liked by farmers. These cars could travel easily on muddy, sandy, or badly rutted country roads. They were light in weight, and the body was high off the ground. No matter how worn out his Model T became, a farmer could usually make it run again with the help of a few tools.

Automobiles changed in appearance in the 1920's. Americans no longer wanted tall cars that looked like buggies. All the large automobile manufacturers began designing cars that were longer and lower than the early ones. Most new models were closed cars so that motorists could be comfortable in any kind of weather. Automobile production increased rapidly after these changes were made.

Early in the twentieth century, manufacturers started to produce trucks and buses. As time went on, buses came to replace trolley cars for transporting people from place to place in the city. (See page 98.) People also began to travel from one city to another by bus. Trucks began to replace wagons pulled by horses on farms and in the city. Then trucks began to compete with railroads for hauling goods from one part of the country to another.

As more and more automobiles, buses, and trucks were built, roads were improved and many new highways were constructed. Today a network of superhighways connects most parts of the United States.

A modern truck. Trucks were first used in large numbers during World War I.*

Because of the automobile, life today is very different from life in America seventy years ago. People do not have to live close to where they work since they can now drive many miles to work in a short time. New shopping malls with large parking lots have taken away much of the business from stores in downtown areas which have less space for parking. Cars have also taken away the business of bus companies and trains. As a result, buses and trains do not run as often as they once did. These changes have made many people depend a great deal on their automobiles. Today many families in the United States have more than one car.

A network of superhighways connects most parts of the United States. Traveling today is easy and pleasant.

The "Savannah" was the first ship to use steam power on a transatlantic* voyage.

18 Ocean Liners and Submarines

One breezy May morning in 1819, a ship sailed out of the harbor of Savannah.* This was the "Savannah," the first vessel to use steam power on a transatlantic* voyage. Black smoke streamed from the smokestack, which was tucked between her billowing white sails. Attached to each of her sides was a large wooden paddle wheel. These wheels were operated by a steam engine inside the ship. As they turned, the ship moved forward.

111

The Savannah was too small to carry much fuel. To save the ship's supply of coal and wood, sails were used most of the time. However, for about four days of the twenty-seven-day trip across the Atlantic Ocean, the steam-powered paddle wheels were used. After the Savannah returned to the United States, its engine was removed. Fuel for the engine took up so much space that there was little room left for cargo. The Savannah ended its days as a sailing vessel.

In April, 1838, another small ship sailed across the Atlantic Ocean. This was the British ship "Sirius." No full, white sails carried the "Sirius" forward. The ship depended entirely on its steam engine. A short distance from New York City, the "Sirius" ran out

The steamship "Washington." Early transatlantic steamers had sails as well as steam engines.

The steamship "Pacific" carried passengers and mail between New York and Liverpool, England.

of fuel. Crew members chopped down the ship's tall, wooden masts to feed the engine's fire. Slowly the "Sirius" steamed into New York Harbor. It had just completed the first entirely steam-powered voyage across the Atlantic Ocean.

American steamships were making regular Atlantic crossings by 1847. They soon took much of the transatlantic passenger and freight trade away from sailing packets.* Sailing vessels often had to wait for favorable winds, but steamships could travel steadily at the same speed hour after hour. By 1850, steamships usually crossed the Atlantic in ten to twelve days.

Many improvements have been made in steamships since the 1850's. Side paddle wheels have been replaced by huge, screw propellers located at the rear of the ship. They drive the ship through the water at such high speeds that the voyage from New York to London can be made in four and a half days. Since 1881, shipbuilders have been using steel for making ships. Steel is stronger than the wood and iron used in earlier ships. Oceangoing ships are now larger as well as stronger. Some are nearly one thousand feet long and carry two thousand passengers.

Today, luxury liners are often used for vacation trips called cruises. Cruise ships are like floating hotels, offering many comforts and conveniences to vacationers. A cruise ship may stop at different ports along its route to allow passengers to go ashore for sightseeing and shopping.

An ocean liner is driven by screw propellers at the stern, instead of by paddle wheels.

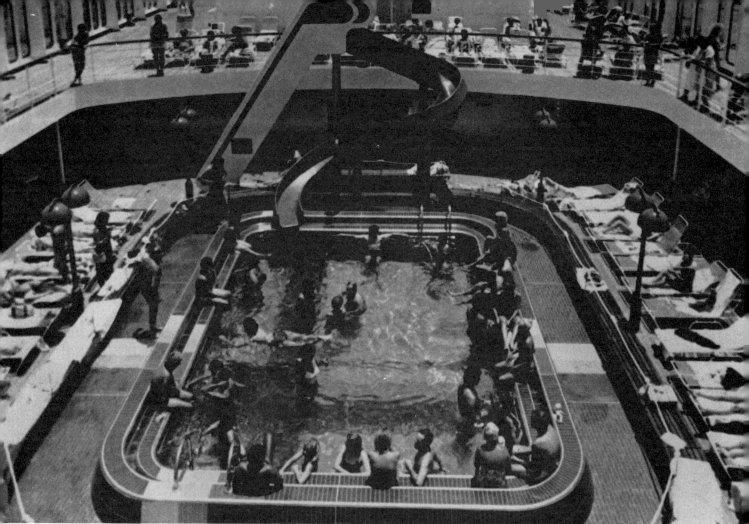

On a cruise ship. Cruise ships are like floating hotels, with swimming pools and restaurants.

For many years before steamships first crossed the ocean, inventors tried to make a ship that could travel under water. It was not until the end of the nineteenth century, however, that a completely successful submarine was built. This submarine was designed by an American, John P. Holland,* and was added to the United States Navy in 1900. Since that time, many larger and better "subs" have been built for our navy.

The submarine has been used mainly for military purposes rather than for transporting passengers or freight. Because it can travel under water, a sub is able to approach and sink an enemy ship without being seen. The crew submerges* the submarine by letting the sea water into tanks that are located between the inner and outer hulls. The subs used in World War II could stay under water for about thirty hours. Then they had to come to the surface to recharge the batteries used to power their engines.

An American submarine was the first ship in the world to be powered by atomic* energy. This is the "Nautilus," which was launched on January 21, 1954. Since then, many other atomic-powered submarines have been built for our navy. Atomic-powered submarines can travel more than twice as fast under water as other submarines. They are able to stay submerged for long periods and can go thousands of miles without refueling. The Trident submarines, which were launched in the 1980's, can travel for nine years before they need to be refueled.

The American submarine "Nautilus" was the first ship to be powered by atomic* energy.

The world's first airplane flight was made by Orville Wright in December, 1903.

19 Travel by Air

For thousands of years, people dreamed of being able to travel through the air like birds. In 1903 this dream came true. Wilbur Wright stood on the windy beach at Kitty Hawk, North Carolina, and watched his brother Orville make the world's first airplane flight. Orville lay on his stomach on a wooden platform that was placed on the lower wing of the plane. Beside him was the small,

An airplane built by the Wright brothers in 1908
could carry a pilot, a passenger, and enough
fuel for an hour of flying.

homemade gasoline engine that powered the airplane's propellers. For twelve seconds, the frail, clumsy little airplane stayed in the air. After a trip of about 120 feet, it settled on the sandy beach. The brothers made three more flights that day. The longest of these lasted only fifty-nine seconds.

The Wright brothers owned a bicycle shop in Dayton, Ohio. They had spent three years experimenting with gliders before they made their engine-driven plane. After their successful flights in 1903, the Wright brothers continued to experiment with airplanes.

Charles A. Lindbergh made the first nonstop flight from New York to Paris in 1927.

The United States government bought its first airplane from Wilbur Wright in 1908. During World War I, American military leaders needed faster airplanes. When the war ended in 1918, airplanes were being built that could fly at speeds of about 150 miles an hour.

Americans were able to travel on regularly scheduled flights by the 1920's. Most travelers, however, preferred to keep their feet on the ground. The small airplanes were fragile, and flying was dangerous.

People became more enthusiastic about air travel after Charles A. Lindbergh made the first nonstop flight from New York to

An early transcontinental* plane. Passengers were transferred to trains for travel at night.

An airport control tower directs plane traffic. Today travel by airplane is safer than by car.

Paris* in 1927.   Lindbergh flew alone in the "Spirit of St. Louis," a small single-engine plane. He flew the 3,900 miles to Paris in thirty-three and one-half hours.

Passengers on the first transcontinental* service, in 1930, flew only during the day. At night they were transferred to trains. The trip took two days and two nights. Only nine passengers could ride

Airplanes at the Dallas-Fort Worth Airport. You can travel to all parts of our country by air.

in each plane. Soon planes were designed that could carry twenty-one passengers across the nation in sixteen hours. Air travel was also made more comfortable. Hot meals were served to passengers during flights.

Many airplanes were used during World War II. Thousands of planes carried soldiers all over the world. Bombers and fighter planes helped win many battles. Airplanes powered by jet* engines were used near the end of the war. Within a few years, these planes were flying faster than the speed of sound.

Today you can travel quickly and safely by air to all parts of the United States and to the major cities of every continent. Perhaps you will ride in a giant supersonic* airplane. Your trip across the Atlantic Ocean will take only four hours. This is less time than it took people to travel from New York to Philadelphia in colonial times. People in other lands have become your neighbors because of air transportation.

Flight attendants on passenger planes serve meals and help the passengers in other ways.

Glossary

Allegheny *(al uh GAY nee)* **Mountains.** A range of mountains in Pennsylvania, Maryland, Virginia, and West Virginia. Part of the Appalachian mountain system. See **Appalachian Mountains.**

Appalachian *(ap uh LAY chun)* **Mountains.** A mountain system in the eastern part of North America. It extends from the Canadian province of Quebec to northern Alabama.

atomic energy. The energy, or force, that is released by the splitting of atoms. Atomic energy produces great heat, which can be used to power machines.

blubber. The fat of whales and other large sea animals.

Boone, Daniel, 1734-1820. American frontiersman. He made two trips of exploration into the Kentucky region, one in 1767 and another in 1769-71. He led settlers into Kentucky in 1775.

chandelier *(shan duh LEER)* . A lighting fixture with several arms or branches that hold candles, gas lights, or electric bulbs. Usually hangs from the ceiling.

charter. To grant certain rights or privileges. Congress gave railroad companies the right to build railroads in the West. It gave them land and loaned them money for this purpose.

cod. One of the most important food fishes. It is caught mainly off the coasts of New England, Newfoundland, and Norway.

Conestoga *(kahn es TOE guh)* **wagon.** A type of covered wagon used in America after the Revolutionary War. Named after the village of Conestoga, Pennsylvania, where they were first made.

corduroy road. A road made with a surface of logs laid side by side across the path. (See picture, page 26.)

diesel- *(DEE zuhl)* **electric locomotive.** A locomotive that is equipped with a diesel engine and an electric generator. The diesel engine runs the generator, which produces the electricity used to power the locomotive. See **diesel engine.**

diesel *(DEE zuhl)* **engine.** A kind of engine that uses fuel oil instead of gasoline for fuel. Named after the German inventor Rudolf Diesel.

dormitory. A sleeping room for a number of people.

Duryea *(DOOR yay)* **brothers.** Charles (1862-1938), called the "father of the automobile," was an inventor. He was assisted by his brother, Frank, who won America's first automobile race, in 1895.

duster. A lightweight overcoat, worn to protect clothing from dust.

Erie Canal. A waterway connecting the Hudson River with Lake Erie. Begun in 1817 and completed in 1825.

Fitch, John, 1743-1798. An American inventor who built the first steamboat in America.

flanged *(FLANJD)* **wheels.** Wheels with rims, such as the wheels of a train. They are designed to keep the train from going off the tracks.

Ford, Henry, 1863-1947. An American automobile manufacturer and inventor. By using assembly-line methods, Ford was able to produce cars at a low price.

Fulton, Robert, 1765-1815. An American engineer and inventor. He built the first commercially successful steamboat, the "Clermont."

Gold Rush. The period in 1848-1849 when the news that gold had been discovered in California brought thousands of people to that state to search for gold.

Griffiths, John Willis, 1809-1882. An American ship designer. Several of his inventions improved the speed and safety of ships.

Holland, John P., 1840-1914. An Irish-American inventor who developed a submarine that operated on electric power when submerged. His first successful submarine, the "Fenian Ram," was launched in 1881. Later he built the "Holland," which was bought by the United States.

Hudson River. A river in New York State, about 306 miles long. It flows southward into the Atlantic Ocean. New York City is located at its mouth. (See map, page 52.)

James River. A river in central Virginia. It flows about 340 miles eastward into Chesapeake Bay. (See map, page 52.)

jet engines. Airplane engines in which burning fuel creates a stream, or jet, of hot gases. These gases shoot out from the rear of the engine and push the plane forward.

mackerel. An important food fish, caught in the North Atlantic.

McKay, Donald, 1810-1880. American designer and builder of clipper ships. He built the finest and fastest ships of his time.

Nantucket. A town on Nantucket Island, off the coast of Massachusetts. (See map, page 52.)

Orient. An old term for the countries of Asia, especially those of eastern Asia.

packet boat. A boat that carried passengers, mail, and freight on scheduled trips.

packet liner. A ship that made regularly scheduled ocean voyages, carrying passengers, mail, and freight.

Paris. The capital and largest city of France.

pitch. A dark, gummy substance that the Indians obtained from balsam or spruce trees and used to seal the seams of their canoes.

Revolutionary War, 1775-1783. The war in which the United States of America won its independence from England.

St. Lawrence River. Flows northeastward from Lake Ontario into the Atlantic Ocean. It forms part of the boundary between the state of New York and Canada. (See map, page 52.)

Santa Fe *(SAN tuh FAY)* **Trail.** An old wagon route from western Missouri to Santa Fe, New Mexico.

Savannah *(suh VAN uh).* A seaport city in southeastern Georgia, at the mouth of the Savannah River.

Schenectady *(skuh NEK tud ee).* An industrial city on the Mohawk River near Albany, New York. (See map, page 52.)

schooner *(SKOON uhr).* A sailing vessel with two or more masts, and special sails that can be handled by a small crew.

Shreve, Henry Miller, 1785-1851. A Mississippi River steamboat captain who designed a steamboat with a special, shallow-bottomed hull, for use on rivers.

Sierra Nevada *(sih EHR uh nuh VAD uh).* A great mountain range located mainly in eastern California. About 430 miles long. Its highest peak, Mount Whitney, is about 14,500 feet high.

staterooms. Private cabins for passengers on board a ship.

submerge. To go under the surface, or to put beneath the surface of the water.

supersonic airplane. An airplane that travels faster than the speed of sound. Sound travels through air at the rate of 1,087 feet per second.

toll. A sum of money which travelers have to pay to use some roads and bridges.

transatlantic. Across or over the Atlantic Ocean.

transcontinental. Going across or reaching across a continent.

velocipede *(vuh LAHS uh peed).* One of the first bicycles. This name was later used for many types of bicycles.

wharf. A structure, usually made of wood or cement, built along the shore of a canal, river, or harbor where boats load and unload freight and passengers.

World War I, 1914-1918. A war that was fought in many parts of the world. On one side were the Central Powers. These were Germany, Austria-Hungary, Turkey, and Bulgaria. They were defeated by the Allies. These included Great Britain, France, Russia, Japan, the United States, and other countries.

World War II, 1939-1945. A war that was fought in many parts of the world. On one side were the Allies, which included the United States, Great Britain, the Soviet Union, France, and many other countries. On the other side were the Axis Powers, which included Germany, Italy, and Japan. The Allies defeated the Axis Powers.

Index

Explanation of abbreviations used in this Index:
p — pictures   *m* — maps

airplanes, 117-123; *p* 117-123
astronauts, 6, 7
automobiles, 105-110; *p* 104-110

Baltimore and Ohio Railroad, 78
barges, 50-51; *p* 48
bicycle clubs, 102; *p* 102
bicycles, 99-103; *p* 99-103
birch-bark canoes, 9-14; *p* 9, 10, 14
boats, 9-14, 22-23, 48-51; *p* 24, 48-50, 53. See also **ships.**
"bobtails," 94; *p* 94
Boone, Daniel, 27
buses, 98, 109, 110; *p* 98

canalboats, 48-51; *p* 48-50
canals, 48-51, 53; *p* 48-50, 53; *m* 52
canoes, 9-14; *p* 9-14
  birch-bark canoes, 9-14; *p* 9, 10, 14
  dugout canoes, 12-13; *p* 11-13
carriages, 18; *p* 18
Central Pacific Railroad, 84-85, 86
China traders, 56-57; *p* 56
city transportation, 91-98; *p* 91-98
"Clermont," 64-66, 68; *p* 64
clipper ships, 59-61; *p* 59, 60, 62
coaches, 18
colonial transportation, 12-13,

15-19, 23-24; *p* 13, 15-19
Concord coaches, 33-34; *p* 34
Conestogas, 39-42; *p* 40, 41
corduroy roads, 26; *p* 26
covered wagons, 36-42; *p* 36-42
Cumberland Road, 29; *m* 52. See also **National Road.**

"De Witt Clinton," 76-77; *p* 76
dugout canoes, 12-13; *p* 11-13
Duryea brothers, 106

early trains, 76-82, 84-88; *p* 76-88
elevated railways, 96-97; *p* 96
Erie Canal, 48-51, 53; *p* 48, 49; *m* 52
explorers, 13

first transcontinental railroad See **transcontinental railroads.**

fishing boats, 22-23; *p* 24
Fitch, John, 66-67; *p* 65,66
flatboats, 43-47; *p* 43-47
"Flying Machines," *p* 32
freight, 72, 73; *p* 73
freight trains, 88-90; *p* 88, 89
Fulton, Robert, 64, 66; *p* 64
fur traders, 13-14; *p* 14

"Great Republic," 61

"hobbyhorse," 100; *p* 100
horse-drawn cars, 78, 79-80; *p* 77, 79

horse-drawn streetcars, 94; *p* 94
horses, 16-17; *p* 15, 16

Indian transportation, 9-12; *p* 10-12

jet planes, 122-123; *p* 122

Lancaster Turnpike, 28-29; *p* 28; *m* 52
Lindbergh, Charles A., 120-121; *p* 119
line boats, 50
locomotives, 76-77, 79-80; *p* 76, 79-85, 87, 88

McKay, Donald, 61; *p* 62
Model T Ford, 107-108; *p* 107
modern trains, 89, 90; *p* 90
motorbuses, 98; *p* 98. See also **buses.**

National Road, 29-30; *p* 30; See also **Cumberland Road.**

127

"Nautilus," 116; *p* 116
"New Orleans," 71

ocean liners, 111-114; *p* 111-114. See also **steamships.**
omnibuses, 91-93; *p* 92, 93
"ordinary," 101-102; *p* 102
"Oriental," 59
oxcarts, 17-18; *p* 17

packet boats, 48-50
packet liners, 55, 57-58; *p* 58
passenger ships, 23-24. See also **canalboats, "Clermont," ocean liners, sailing ships,** and **steamboats.**
postriders, 16; *p* 16
prairie schooners. See **covered wagons.**

railroads, 76-90; *p* 76-90
"Rainbow," 61
river steamers, 70-75; *p* 68-75
roads, early, 25-30; *p* 25-30

"safety" bicycle, 102; *p* 99
sailcars, 78; *p* 78
sailing ships, 20-24, 55-58; *p* 20-24, 54-56, 58. See also **clipper ships** and **schooners.**

"Savannah," 111-112; *p* 111
schooners, 23, 61-63; *p* 23-24, 63
shipbuilding, 21-23; *p* 22
  fishing boats, 22-23
  passenger ships, 23
ships, 20-24, 55-75, 111-116; *p* 20-24, 54-56, 58-60, 62-75, 111-116. See also **boats.**
shipyards, 21-22; *p* 22
Shreve, Henry, 71-72
"Sirius," 112-113
sleighs, 18-19; *p* 19
Soo Canals, 53; *p* 53
space travel, 6-7; *p* 7
"Spirit of St. Louis," 120-121; *p* 119

stagecoaches, 31-35; *p* 31-35
stage wagons, 33; *p* 32
steamboat races, 74; *p* 74
steamboats, 64-75; *p* 64-75
steam locomotives, 76-77, 78-80; *p* 76, 79-85, 87, 88
steamships, 111-114; *p* 111-114
submarines, 115-116; *p* 116
subways, 97; *p* 97
supersonic airplanes, 123

tandem bicycles, 103; *p* 103
"Tin Lizzie," 107-108; *p* 107

toll roads, 27-29; *p* 28, 29
"Tom Thumb," 79-80; *p* 79
trading ships, 56-57; *p* 56
trains, 76-90; *p* 76-90
  early, 76-88; *p* 76-88
  modern, 89-90; *p* 89-90
transcontinental railroads, 83-86, 88; *p* 83-85
transcontinental air service, 121-122, 123; *p* 120-123
trolley cars, 95; *p* 95
trucks, 109; *p* 109

Union Pacific Railroad, 84-86; *p* 83, 84

"velocipede," 100-101; *p* 101

wagon train, 36-38; *p* 36-38
"Washington," 71-72
westward migration, 34-38, 41-46, 88; *p* 35-39, 42-46, 84-88
whaling, 20-21; *p* 20
Wilderness Road, 27; *p* 27; *m* 52
World War I, 120
World War II, 116, 122-123
Wright brothers, 117-120; *p* 117, 118